JENNIFER LYN
POEMS

JENNIFER LYN
POEMS

JENNIFER COMBELLACK

ARCHWAY
PUBLISHING

Archway Publishing books may be ordered through booksellers or by contacting:

Archway Publishing
1663 Liberty Drive
Bloomington, IN 47403
www.archwaypublishing.com
844-669-3957

ISBN: 978-1-6657-5046-2 (sc)
ISBN: 978-1-6657-5045-5 (hc)
ISBN: 978-1-6657-5047-9 (e)

Library of Congress Control Number: 2023918158

Print information available on the last page.

Archway Publishing rev. date: 10/16/2023

DEDICATION

I dedicate this book of poetry to my American queens,
Ava Amelia and Quinci Belle, and to my winged king, Calvin.
I love you more than my words can express.

I'm Jennifer Lyn Combellack, momma, poet, and teacher, riding the waves of life. I find my inspiration in the profound and intricate tapestry of life itself. Through my poetry, I explore the multifaceted aspects of existence, delving into the realms of love, life, grief, nature, and the eternal circle of life.

As a mother, I draw from the wellspring of emotions and experiences that come with nurturing and witnessing the growth of a child. The boundless love and devotion that define motherhood fuel my verses on love, encapsulating the beauty and complexity of human connections.

As a teacher, I've been granted the privilege of guiding young minds, instilling knowledge and curiosity. This role has deepened my appreciation for the ebb and flow of life's lessons, inspiring me to craft verses that reflect the transformative power of education and self-discovery.

Grief, an inevitable part of existence, has also found its place in my poetry. I use my words to navigate the depths of sorrow and find solace in the healing journey. My verses serve as a reminder that even in the darkest of times, there is a glimmer of hope and resilience.

Nature, with its boundless beauty and ceaseless cycles, has always been a wellspring of inspiration. I paint vivid landscapes with my words, capturing the splendor of the natural world and its intricate interplay with our lives.

Lastly, I explore the timeless concept of the circle of life. Through my poetry, I celebrate the continuity of existence, finding solace in the idea that life is a perpetual, ever-turning wheel.

In essence, I am Jennifer Lyn Combellack, a momma, a poet, and a teacher who is driven to write by the intricate and ever-evolving tapestry of love, life, grief, nature, and the eternal circle of existence. My verses are a reflection of the profound beauty and complexity that define the human experience. Together, we ride the waves of life, exploring its depths and celebrating its heights through the power of poetry.

CONTENTS

AMERICAN QUEENS

American queens,
Such a gorgeous ring.
Fond thoughts when we'd sing,
Our kin with a dream.
Appreciate all;
Sail through that wall.
Work hard for reward,
The dream we go toward.
These gold-rush roots creep
Generations deep.
Been raised up humble,
Strength in the struggle.
Please fly on your wings,
The nature of things.
Passing on your crown,
Bright lineage down.
Teach lessons to live,
Service you can give.
Heartfelt gratitude,
Always lifts one's mood.
Respect where we came,
Unique none the same.
Connected we dream,
Continue to sing.
You're gorgeous beings,
American queens.

MAGNOLIA SPIRIT

To our river we run.
Cloud blanket covers sun.
Feet on leather-hard clay,
Snowflake wisdom will say.
Unique flakes ripple out.
River rhythms about.
Experiences true.
Always feel charged with you.
I know you can feel it,
Magnolia spirit.

BUTTERFLY YOU

Chrysalis cradles deep growth.
Heart and mind, I love you both.
New perspective every day,
Silence in the words I say.
Gracefully ride these waves, please.
Prayers up bring me to my knees.
Blazing trails unique to me.
Yes, she is a queen, you see.
Memories are engraved here.
Choose loyalty when you steer.
True self-love from inside out.
Stay the course with strength and clout.
Brand-new chapter breaks on through.
Fly so free, butterfly you.

BE BRIGHT

Gotta love our amazing Cali.
From the turquoise sea to the glitterin' Sierra,
All in a day.
Gotta love these charging waves,
Connection ancient and overflows our cups.
Listen to what I gotta say.
Gotta love miraculous metamorphosis.
Plugged in, please hold my hand.
All I wanna do is play.
Gotta love infinite space.
Breath in and out our atmosphere.
Be bright as sun's ray.

EPIPHANIES

Don't know what the future brings.
Epiphanies, my heart sings.
Be yourself, be true and wild.
See the world, eyes of a child.
Renewal restarts our Earth.
Wear your smile, and love your worth.
Rain nourishes, flower grows,
Peace inside, inner joy glows.
Don't know what the future brings.
Epiphanies, my heart sings.

NEST

Grateful for nest, cozy and warm,
Perfect place to shelter the storm.
Peace inside, deep river runs pure,
Electric love radiates cure.
We pray to those who guide us,
Perched upon your golden truss.
I'm always here to reassure,
Warrior princess, not demure.
Present is gift in infinite form.
Grateful for nest, cozy and warm.

UP

Unique people looking up.
Peaceful home fills golden cup.
Love friends and family the same.
Stardust lights our flame.
Souls' energies infinite gain,
Protected from wind and rain.
Animals are far from tame.
Always call me by my name.
Joy overflows golden cup.
Unique people looking up.

REST

Rest is the beat without sound.
Golden heart is treasure found.
Eloquent pictures words paint.
Breath gifts patience to a saint.
Reminds us to be here now,
So naturally we know how.
Comfort in muse's embrace;
Pure joy in that smiling face.
I am authentically me.
Life is the music we see.
Golden heart is treasure found.
Rest is the beat without sound.

INFINITE FRIEND

Infinite friend,
Forever and always,
Past the end.
We run in the hallways,
Convos deep,
Never ever speechless.
Secrets keep,
Beauty breathless.
Please let confidence seep.
Por vida,
You will constantly steer.
Queen Diva,
Infinite friend is here.

SPRINGING

Love and serenity
Fill my being.
Magnets attract me,
Feathers freeing.
Authentic one you see,
Peace I'm bringing.
Beaming, just breathe and be.
Music singing,
Flowing in key.
Rhythm beats forth springing.

BECOMING

Becoming human right before my eyes,
Truly authentic with infinite tries.
Only the truth, no need for messy lies,
Built strong to last, much grander than all size.
Diamond-like rarity, most perfect prize,
Life hands out lessons; happy tears she cries.
Truly authentic with infinite tries,
Becoming human right before my eyes.

CELESTIAL BOW

Song sings of intellectual one.
Perspective feels love and fun.
Don't mistake this rarity;
Unique being you do see.
Foundation rock-solid true,
This strength magnetizes you.
Shed all the fear that holds back.
Self-love keeps us all on track.
Breathe in peace, we feel light.
Source flows free morning 'til night.
Release and let go right now.
All is well, celestial bow.
Song sings of intellectual ones,
Lyrics of stars, moons, and suns.

VOICE

Wise woman's voice in my ear.
Perspectives filtered I hear.
Close your eyes; take deep breath in.
Live authentically to win.
Exude bright light and love true.
Just be whoever is you.
Gifts we share are genuine.
The comfort in one's own skin.
Moments in time, pray we steer.
Wise woman's voice in my ear.

SEES

Springing forth all inner joy,
Helping others, noble ploy.
Honest, dedicated, bright,
Levity in safety right.
Empath nurtures our true soul,
Infinite abundance whole.
Walk alone together path.
Bubble keeps out downing wrath.
Consciousness lifts us up now,
Knowing our true self is how.
Graceful flight on lovely breeze,
Hummingbird glows, worth she sees.

GLISTEN

Glisten reflects, ripples gleam.
River's waters wash her clean.
Monarch adventures today;
Wings always flutter her way.
Life springs forth from sacred banks,
Surrender on breeze, give thanks.
Carry her to new places.
See all beautiful faces.
Nature pulses through our veins.
River flows so fresh with rains.
Glisten reflects, ripples gleam.
River's waters wash her clean.

OCEAN SONG

Ocean, hear me sing my song.
Wave after wave, always strong.
Consistency charges all,
There to catch us when we fall.
Walking this life, grateful heart,
Knew I loved you from the start.
Mountain warrior, it's true.
Miraculous right on cue.
Absorb precious moments now.
Every effort, show you how.
Transparent, my walls are down.
Ocean's jewels, glittery crown.
Seek and you shall find you know
All colors of the rainbow.
Inner circle so complete,
Full moon cycle on repeat.
Nature loves us in all seasons.
My babies are my reasons.
Wave after wave, always strong.
Ocean, hear me sing my song.

BRAVE BUILD

Brave soul, breathe, and just let it be.
All our wildest dreams we see.
Released you, and you flew away;
There was no need for you to stay.
Sacred ground, ancient in power,
Stand tall; there's nowhere to cower.
This shared human experience,
Trauma changes, not the same since.
Feel beauty in the struggle.
Who would we be without trouble?
Pain and joy, we do ride these waves.
Love rises, infinitely saves.
Lean in, put heartbeat to my ear,
Rhythmical drumbeat I can hear.
Yes, we are here, and we are free.
Build a beautiful life with me.

FOCUS

Mindful hearts will fly.
Focus, Eagle Eye.
Calm before the storm,
Far above the norm.
Soar on wings with strength
For infinite length.
Vantage point sees eye.
Happy tears to cry,
Nurturing rainfall.
Nature, hear my call.
Faith in every word.
Butterflies, free bird.
Mindful hearts will fly.
Focus, Eagle Eye.

OCEAN LOVE

Absolutely magical trip.
The ocean mist upon our lips.
Night after night,
The stars shine bright.
We see waves wash upon the shore.
Worth the wait, always wanting more.
Day after day,
We laugh and play.
Majestic redwoods high above,
Magical memories, ocean love.

TIME TRAVEL

We time travel through our mind,
Coastal camping to unwind.
Reconnect, one of a kind,
Beautiful treasures we find.
Perfect bench, sun, moon, and sea,
Nowhere that we'd rather be.
Opened our eyes, and we see
Magic memories, you and me.
Eucalyptus forest home,
Road trip—the best way to roam.
Infinite beaches to comb.
Inspired to write a poem.
Unlocked hearts with pure-gold key,
Sleeping underneath our tree.
Absolute, we guarantee,
Nowhere that we'd rather be.

PRESENCE

Drinking coffee by super moonlight,
King's presence makes everything all right.
Walking this path, a most faithful fate,
High on life since our very first date.
Dancing in the rain, feel the groove,
Perfect music notes hit, and we move.
Shooting stars fly as gaze lifts us up.
These magic moments fill our cup.
Enjoying this gift of love and light,
King's presence makes everything all right.

PERFECT PASSION

Perfect circles just for you,
Passion fuses, joining two.
Fanning flames burn ever hot,
Forever found special spot.
Victory is always ours.
Vida is strength in powers.
Infinity flows from here,
Eye of God, no need to steer.
Moment unmatched our first kiss.
Magical seeds planted bliss.
Wander up and down the coast,
Warrior, to you I toast.
Perfect circles drawn in sand,
Passion fuses joining hands.

WIND AND WAVES

Wind blows blades of grass.
Through our minds, thoughts pass.
Salty sea surround;
Coastal waves abound.
Graceful birds in flight,
Embraces feel right.
Time ticks as blood pumps.
Butterflies, heart jumps.
Hold me close, my dear.
In our strength, no fear.
See turquoise water.
Truly, you got her.
From the dark, light saves.
Love to ride all waves.

ANGELS AND RAVENS

Angels and ravens, playing our song.
Connection strong, no matter how long.
Water trickles, physics feels good.
The truth is so right; do what you should.
Freshest of air fills our being.
These perfect miracles we're seeing.
While running and playing, here to stay,
Always thinking of the words to say.
The gratitude that fills our heart.
Wings bring us together, never part.
Fly on this early morning breeze.
All prayers answered when brought to our knees.
Angels and ravens playing our song,
Connection strong, no matter how long.

ROYAL ENLIGHTEN

As senses heighten,
Royal enlighten.
I sit here and pray
With nothing to say.
Time to listen in.
Only want a win.
Perfect place to be,
It's nature and me.
Hear feathers in flight
Only feels right.
Sweetest air on Earth,
Strength in knowing worth.
Own breath hits my tongue.
New day starts so young.
River flows through us,
All superfluous.
Prayers answered each day,
Silent words to say.
As senses heighten,
Royal enlighten.

STILL

He said time will tell
Because time stood still.
Feel it; all is well
'Cause he said he will.
Bloom, outta my shell
Because time stood still.
All natural, no sell,
'Cause I said I will.
Listen for the bell
Because time stood still.
Head over heels fell,
'Cause we said we will.

IRON HORSE

Iron horse pulls into the station.
Perfect getaway, love vacation.
Two grateful hearts connect as sparks fly,
Rivers and trails and infinite sky.
Lifetime of sights as these lovers leap,
Bodies wrapped up in most comfortable sleep.
Such perfect meals, our souls they nourish,
Time spent together, we always cherish.
Perfect getaway, love vacation.
Iron horse pulls into the station.

SACRED SPACE

Holding this sacred space around our love,
Gratitude in faith and strength above.
Infinite memories stored in mind.
Wrapped in golden light, seek, and ye shall find.
Heart wide open; walls have been torn down.
Learning life places jewels in our crown.
Travel to worlds beyond most vivid dreams.
Close your eyes and listen: sky, birds, and streams.
Waking to perfect sunrise, brand-new day,
Truly listening to words that we say.
Together we will walk into the sunset,
Exciting levels beyond all reached yet.
Gratitude in faith and strength above,
Holding this sacred space around our love.

AMORE, SHE FALLS

Time tears down these castle walls.
Pick up, no matter the falls.
We always have ourselves.
Grab our hearts off these shelves.
Happiness is found inside.
Hold on for life's wild ride.
Soldier on; we can do it.
Try our best, we never quit.
Love conquers all, truth prevails,
Breeze blows wind into our sails.
We're up here, higher than walls,
Never fear, amore she falls.

IDEAL YOU

Ideal right here, right now.
Consistent waves show you how.
Keep your head up; breathe fresh air.
Strength in heart, absorb love's stare.
History roots, anchored ground,
Ocean plays lullaby's sound.
Tide comes in and goes back out.
With grace, obstacles surmount.
See no need to swim upstream.
Float with the flow, smiles beam,
Can't hold back feelings so true.
Always in my heart is you.

PERFECT PATH

Perfect path, humble and strong,
Pure surrender, sing our song.
Embrace with graceful kindness.
Rise challenge, seek uniqueness.
Loyal bond, tie above all,
Represent crown, power call.
Ethereal being here,
Higher one will always steer.
Pure surrender, sing our song,
Perfect path, humble and strong.

COVER

Blanket of stars, take my cover.
Heavenly thoughts, you are lover.
Under ancients, infinite light,
Always have me, one who is bright.
Guiding this star, never will part,
Adoration, pure from the start.
Tune out static, sole harmony,
Distance never too far from me.
Deep strength in faith, this bond of steal,
Magic souls fuse lifetimes of real.
Heavenly thoughts, you are lover,
Blanket of stars, take my cover.

WILD RIDE

Patient wild ride,
Always on flip side.
Shadow comes to play,
What she wants to say.
Healed deep trauma,
Always your momma.
Stay strong in power.
Shooting stars shower.
This moonlight dances,
Infinite chances.
All her lessons learned,
Magical ways churned.
Laughing light with joy,
Muscle heart, not toy.
Protect, armor down,
See her glowing crown.
Breath fills this being,
Unique one seeing.
Always on flip side,
Patient wild ride.

ELEVEN ELEVEN WIN

Eleven eleven win,
Soak up this warm sun on skin.
To manifest what you want,
Ask yourself, one's confidant.
Dream upon dream will come true,
See this believer in you.
Wildest adventures think
Shooting star is just a blink.
Absolutely known as fact,
Soulmates connect, sacred pact.
Loyal would do anything;
Perfect words forever ring.
Soulmates connect, sacred pact,
Absolutely known as fact.
Shooting star is just a blink,
Wildest adventures think.
See this believer in you.
Dream upon dream will come true.
Ask yourself, one's confidant,
To manifest what you want.
Soak up this warm sun on skin,
Eleven eleven win.

PRAY

Breath fills up silence to say,
Feeling so peace filled today.
True me is outta my way.
Blessed, it's powerful to pray.
Gratitude for every day,
Go with the flow, as it may.
All this self-love clears the way.
Grace, it's fulfilling to pray.
Perfect pieces as they lay,
Goodness is the price I pay.
On my path, I find my way.
Integrity, I do pray.
Breath fills up, silence to say,
Feeling so peace-filled today.
True me is outta my way.
Blessed, it's powerful to pray.

EAGLE EYE

Such magnificent beauty,
Gorgeous everywhere we see.
Emerald pools rain down on us.
Perfect pace, breathe, never rush.
Eagles play on gentle breeze,
Nature's canvas to our knees.
Grateful for every moment,
Magic space where all time went.
Completely right, changed our lives,
Sandstone walls where eagle dives.
Read our minds, know what we mean,
Eagle eye, be what we've seen.

NATURE LOVER

These words hold me in their embrace,
My rhyme and reason beyond face.
Much deeper than chasms echo,
Epiphanies, and then you know.
Brings a cleansing through winter storm,
Grateful heart inside cozy home.
On these strong winds fall leaves take flight.
Good souls are action, always right.
We're finding answers in the heart.
It's faith connection where we start.
Thankfully, life is a circle,
Learning to uncover worth all.
Never judging books by cover,
Grounding earth to nature lover.

WEIGHT

We feel the weight of our song,
Known it infinitely long.
Each note anchors us to earth,
Singing lyrics of self-worth.
As this river of sound flows,
Stay in our power; it shows.
Observing all in the zone,
Look inside miracles shown.
Perfect harmony we shift,
Living life's beautiful gift.
Known it infinitely long,
We feel the weight of our song.

MIRACULOUS MESSAGES

Magical beauty everywhere,
Forever see you in my stare.
With every wave crashing on shore,
Inside souls heal evermore.
Total embrace protects us all,
Love envelops, hear nature's call.
Bald eagle, red tail, hummingbird,
Miraculous messages heard.
Brave storms' winds with feet planted here,
Present's gifts abundantly clear.
Forever see you in my stare,
Magical beauty everywhere.

SUN GLITTERS

Sun glitters on the Tennessee River.
Head to your toes, you can feel that shiver.
Full send of that magic up through your spine,
Countryside changes you, makes you all mine.
The deepest of love flows in that current.
Its message received, you know you heard it.
Feathers float free on these gale-force winds.
Scent is the sweetest, and your mind it sends.
Talons, like knives, through beak send out your call,
Flying so high, impossible to fall.
Light of full moon always guides us on home,
Core of the soul, wherever we may roam.
Sunup to sundown, this growth is immense.
Ethereal connect, not the same since.
Head to your toes, you can feel that shiver.
Sun glitters on the Tennessee River.

SECOND NATURE

Your name's on my lips, second nature.
Your kisses are my favorite flavor.
Forever memories of our time,
Favorite place, arms woven, yours and mine.
A relaxing space on coastal drive,
These two beating hearts feel so alive.
Knowing every moment etched in stone,
Essence lives never truly alone.
With faith intact, these waves wash us clean.
Genuine truth, we say what we mean.
Your kisses are my favorite flavor.
Your name's on my lips, second nature.

ACCEPTANCE DANCE

Brick-wall acceptance,
This life is a dance.
All complex features,
Loving Earth's creatures.
When fresh breath flows in,
I am Jennie Lyn.
Complete heart expands,
Holding future hands.
True gift is right here,
A happiness tear.
Past brings deep wisdom,
A gratitude Mom.
Waves come, and they go.
Thank you, magic show.
Connect in exhale,
Told in my tale.
Every single crease
Creates headpiece.
This life is a dance.
Brick-wall acceptance.

BRILLIANT

Brilliant magic moon lights our way.
Owl tells us what we need to say.
Gives us energy, here and now.
These perfect feelings show us how.
Sound travels through crisp winter air.
Wise owl and moon are quite the pair.
Dreams travel deeply through our stare.
Words and actions, infinite care.
These perfect moments show us how.
Gives us life, here and now.
Owl tells us what we need to say.
Brilliant magic moon lights our way.

VICARIOUS

Our nest, cozy warm,
Protected from storm.
Rest, love, meditate.
Gratitude so great.
Joy vicarious,
Soul mysterious.
This infinite one,
Imagination.
Closed eyes, here I am,
Strong winds kiss my hands.
Imagination,
This infinite one.
Smile delicious,
Taste vicarious.
Magic featherweight,
Heart, love, heal it.
Protected from storm,
Our nest, cozy warm.

HEART

Has my heart from now until the end.
Journey around the next river bend.
Feel so alive as rain trickles down;
Precipitation absorbs through crown.
The freshest of air fills our lungs.
Joyful laughter toward heaven on tongues.
As we live and breathe, blessings our gifts,
Rapids are ridden, energy shifts.
The fullest of moons light up our way
With infinite, love-filled words to say.
Forests and flowers, dirt path at feet,
Here souls connect, where we'll always meet.
Journey around the next river bend,
Has my heart from now until the end.

OUR SONG

My head rests on your perfect chest,
Rhythm of heart, beating the best.
We know dreams really do come true
In our own world, me and you.
This complete embrace, hand in hand,
Walking with our toes in the sand.
Under the forest boughs above,
Sharing souls of infinite love.
As our song plays on strings and keys,
Thank you, God, bring me to my knees.
Rhythm of heart beating the best,
My head rests on your perfect chest.

GOLDEN SUN

Golden sun warms the frost-bowed buttercups.
Trail thaws as ice turns to fresh raindrops.
Three bluebirds play on feathers like the sky,
Absorb vicariously in mind's eye.
With heart at ease in the freshest of air,
Always so grateful that you heard my prayer.
Mighty river flows, watch waves ebb and flow,
This life is a gift that open eyes show.
Trail thaws as ice turns to fresh raindrops,
Golden sun warms the frost-bowed buttercups.

CLEAR

Angel wings clear our path,
Protected from the wrath.
Surrounded with pure love,
Watching out up above.
Ethereal light shines,
Illuminates our minds.
Lead us not into it;
Temptation does not fit.
In white feather embrace,
Infinite smile on face.
Protected from the wrath,
Angel wings clear our path.

ETHEREAL SPACE

Sun, warm on my face,
Ethereal space.
Gratitude in heart,
Where I always start.
Life lessons we learn,
True wisdom we earn.
With faith in this trail,
Feel strong wind in sail.
Oath of honesty,
Loyal core of me.
Heaven and Earth hold,
Magic tale told.
River navigate,
Time never too late.
Absorb ups and downs,
Turning smiles from frowns.
Silence is teacher,
Quietest reach her.
Infinite connect,
Imperfect perfect.
Pure joy on my face,
Ethereal space.

PERFECT NATURE

All the good feels here.
Sun, dirt, river steer.
Birds' songs float through air,
Perfect nature stare.
Kindness in this heart,
Breathe in favorite part.
Experience all.
Get up after fall.
Determination
Is the foundation.
Love is where we fall.
Joy will soak up all.
Pure souls never part,
Knowledge in this heart.
Perfect nature stare,
Birds' songs float through air.
Sun, dirt, river steer.
All the good feels here.

WATERS' WAVES

These waters' waves, so pure and true,
Gift to walk this path with you.
Embrace me, warm river dune.
Sweet notes float in complete tune.
Fully present, here and now,
Experience shows you how.
Strength in solitude feels good,
Occurs exactly as should.
These perfect prints on worn trail,
Consistent universe mail.
Outside, beyond all those walls,
Bridges traverse waterfalls.
Tiny wildflowers greet;
Sandy beach is comfy seat.
Please take me here every time,
Even journey in my mind.
Gift to walk this path with you,
These waters' waves, so pure and true.

SIGN

Prayer, "Please God, help me,"
Sends a sign to see.
Sun emerges bright,
Heaven's clouds in sight.
Gentle winds through hair,
Tranquil water stare.
Strength to stand my ground,
Peace inside I've found.
Let it all go now.
In good faith I bow.
Simply rooted here,
Angels always near.
Dance river, glisten.

I forever listen.
Breathe that willow scent.
Souls flow where they went.
Wings to fly so free
Sends a sign to me.

DEAR OCEAN

Dear ocean I love,
When push comes to shove,
You have my heart now,
A forever vow.
Every breath of you
Recharged anew.
Riding all-white waves,
Cyclical tide saves.
Seals play in the surf,
Most beautiful turf.
Birds soar with the wind,
Infinite joy brimmed.
Out past horizon,
Warm sun is risen.
Schools of fish glisten.
Melodic, listen,
A forever vow.
You have my heart now,
When push comes to shove,
Dear ocean I love.

HEAVENLY WISH

Heavenly wish,
Great egret, fish.
Foggy mist envelops me,
White wings' serendipity.
Magic in air,
Honest and fair.
Ocean tide nourishes all.
Soul connects, I heard your call.
Porthole window,
Beyond we know,
Opens up this perspective.
Truly thankful gift to live.
Riding all waves,
Maritime gift saves.
Look up, please God, help me.
White wings' serendipity.
Great egret, fish.
Heavenly wish.

LOYAL LOVE

Mine is a loyal love,
One sent from light above.
Only you in my mind,
A unique find.
A treasured heart of gold,
Red, white, and blue in bold.
Around me wrap your limbs.
Hear sounds of angel hymns.
Safe, at ease, always you,
Wishes and dreams come true.
Know I let my walls down
Whenever you're around.
Heaven and Earth we sing,
Highest happiness bring.
One sent from light above,
Ours is a loyal love.

Printed in the United States
by Baker & Taylor Publisher Services